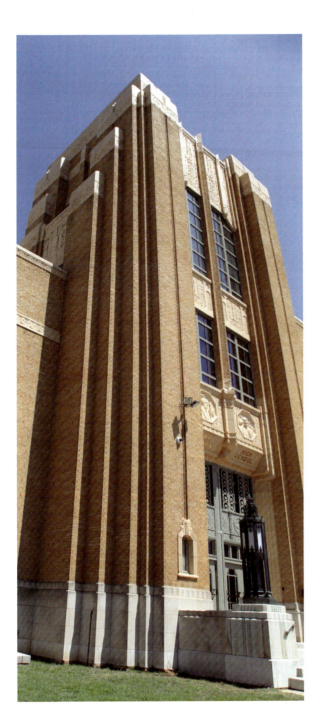

HIGH S

"While attending Will Rogers High School as a young teen, I had no idea that I was going to school in a work of art." — Don Wagner (Class of 1965)

**Copyright 2013,
Oklahoma Tourist Guides Inc.,
All Rights Reserved**

All rights reserved under international and Pan-American copyright conventions. No part of this publication can be reproduced, stored in a retrieval system, or transmitted by any form, or by any means electronic, mechanical, photocopying, recording or otherwise, without prior written permission of the copyright owner.

Published by :

OKLAHOMA TOURIST GUIDES

Oklahoma Tourist Guides Inc.
www.Tulsa-Books.com
(918) 693-1198
DON.WAGNER.OK@GMAIL.COM

Introduction

Will Rogers High Schools is a beautiful school with a historic tradition. Every student who attends Roger is impacted uniquely by their experiences. I have my own. I attended Will Rogers from the Fall of 1962 - Spring of 1965. Those three years created the foundation for the rest of my life. It is where I found my first love, future wife and mother to my four children. Needless to say I have fond memories of Will Rogers and I want to share with others all the unique facilities and rich history that makes it more than just another school.

This book covers many aspects of Will Rogers High School and Junior High School, but due to space limitations can't cover everything in the detail it deserves.

Some of the topics incorporated in the book include:

- The building of the High School
- Historical Timelines of Significant Events
- School Symbolism
- School Traditions
- Architecture
- Interior Decoration
- Famous Alumni
- Myths and Legends
- Will Rogers Photographs
- National Register of Historic Places

Come and explore with me the intriguing facts, stories and myths about Will Rogers High School.

Southwest entrance to the school

My Special Thanks !!!
People who contributed to this book.

Mary Ellen Strakoulas
Mary Ellen edits my books and keeps me straight when my thoughts wander. When times get tough, she is always there to encourage and support me.

Seed Technologies and Tony Lyons (Class of 1994)
Seed Technologies is an outstanding web design and software development firm that designs stunning websites optimized for businesses. Tony designed and created the book covers.

Joann Lewis (Class of 1955)
Joann provided assistance in reviewing the book for historical discrepancies. Having her fresh set of eyes on the editorial content was very valuable.

Jan Weinheimer (Class of 1966)
Jan designed and created pages for the Will Rogers High School All Sports Booster Club and the Will Rogers High School Community Foundation. A special thanks goes to Jan for helping proof the book to identify typos, grammatical and technical errors.

Table of Contents

Publishers Page	1
Introduction	2
Table of Contents	3
Will Rogers High School	4
Will Rogers the Man and Legend	5
Historical Timelines	6
The Beginnings	14
The Architects	15
The School Design	16
Construction	17
Details Make a Masterpiece	18
School Opens	20
School Symbolism	22
Student Life	24
Instrumental Music	27
Student Athletics	28
The "Round Up" & "Lariat"	30
Patriotism & Veterans Memorials	32
Will Rogers Photo Collection	34
Introduction to Art Deco	36
Exterior Designs	38
Will Rogers & Education Panels	46
Art Deco Interior	48
West Foyer	50
Main Hall	52
The Library	54
East Foyer	56
Auditorium Foyer	58
Auditorium	60
The Rindskopf Mural	66
Famous Will Rogers Alumni	68
Will Roger s Foundation	72
Alumni Websites	73
National Register of Historic Places	74
Restoration & Improvement Projects	75
Will Rogers College High School	76
Will Rogers Public Tours	78
Recommended Data Sources	79
Other Tulsa Books	80

Art Deco vents in the SE & SW school entry porticos

Will Rogers High School

Art Deco Lantern lighting for auditorium steps

In the mid-1930's, the Tulsa Board of Education, with assistance from the Public Works Administration (PWA), began construction on two high schools, originally named East Side and West Side. "East Side" was renamed before construction to "Will Rogers High School" where as West Side became "Daniel Webster High School". In 1936, the school board purchased nearly 29 acres of pasture from the Fred Turner family for $21,772.

Shortly after his death, the school was named Will Rogers High School. The name had a definite impact on the architectural design of the building. Joseph Koberling and Leon Senter sought to make the school a functional monument and memorial to the popular humorist. They sought to make the building both attractive and functional by implementing 101 design features. Their goal was to develop a school that projected a lively and joyous environment, like the personality of Will Rogers. They beautifully integrated the modern architecture of the day with quality materials and first-class craftsmanship.

The school opened in September of 1939 with an enrollment of 1501 students. Shortly after opening Rogers High School was featured in a *Time Magazine* article "outlining the high school pattern of the future." The school was called "a model progressive high school" in "one of the most progressive school systems in the study."

Will Rogers High School, designed by Leon B. Senter and Joseph R. Koberling, Jr., has exterior art-deco Zig-Zag features. The interior displays a great deal of craftsmanship artistry throughout the building. Tulsa Public Schools financed the building with a 45% PWA grant. Therefore the building is designated a PWA Art Deco Styled building.

The National Park Service recognizes Will Rogers High School as one of the best examples of Art Deco high school architecture in the country. In 2007, the building was added to the National Register of Historic Places as a location of national significance.

Today Will Rogers College High School occupies the building. Students attend from grades 6 through 12 and can graduate with a College Associates Degree.

Will Rogers the Man and Legend

Painted portrait found in the auditorium foyer

Will Rogers is Oklahoma's favorite son. He was born on November 4, 1879 on the Rogers Ranch near Oologah, in what was then Indian Territory. He was of partial Cherokee descent and grew up working on the family ranch.

He began his entertainment career as "The Cherokee Kid" in the "Texas Jack's Wild West Show." He became so talented with a rope that he was listed in the Guinness Book of World Records for roping three moving horses simultaneously. He even performed in the 1904 World's Fair in St. Louis.

By 1917, he was performing vaudeville with the Ziegfeld Follies. It was a mixture of a roping exhibition and a stand up comedy routine where he made amusing observations about people, politics and government in a homespun folksy manner. This led to his acting career.

In 1918, Will starred in several silent films like Laughing Bill Hyde (1918) and The Ropin' Fool (1921). Will became a national celebrity with the advent of talking films like "They Had to See Paris (1929) and State Fair (1934). His folksy country drawl had wide audience appeal. Rogers starred in 71 films and Broadway productions. By 1934, he was the top leading man in Hollywood.

Will was a multi- media superstar. He wrote over 4,000 nationally syndicated newspaper columns. He wrote satirically about government, politics and politicians. He also wrote six books and became a prominent radio broadcaster. His intelligent observations presented in a humorous way made him the nation's top political commentator and probably the most beloved individual in the country.

Will stayed out of politics, preferring to stand on the side lines and make fun of the government, politicians and political parties. He even declined a nomination to run for governor of Oklahoma. Will was friends of Presidents Calvin Coolidge and Franklin Roosevelt as well as most of the prominent people of his time.

In 1935, at the age of 55, Will Rogers died in an airplane crash in Point Barrow, Alaska on August 15, 1935. He was on a private plane piloted by aviator, Wiley Post. Will's wife, Betty built the Will Rogers Memorial on land in Claremore. The memorial museum was dedicated in 1938, by President Franklin D. Roosevelt. In 1944, Will's remains were moved to the Claremore memorial.

Will Rogers was America's first multi-media super star providing humorous national commentary. His radio program was the model for the "Tonight Show" monologue. Rogers was the most widely read newspaper columnist and had the highest rated weekly radio show in the country. In addition Rogers was a hugely popular movie star and Americas most beloved celebrity.

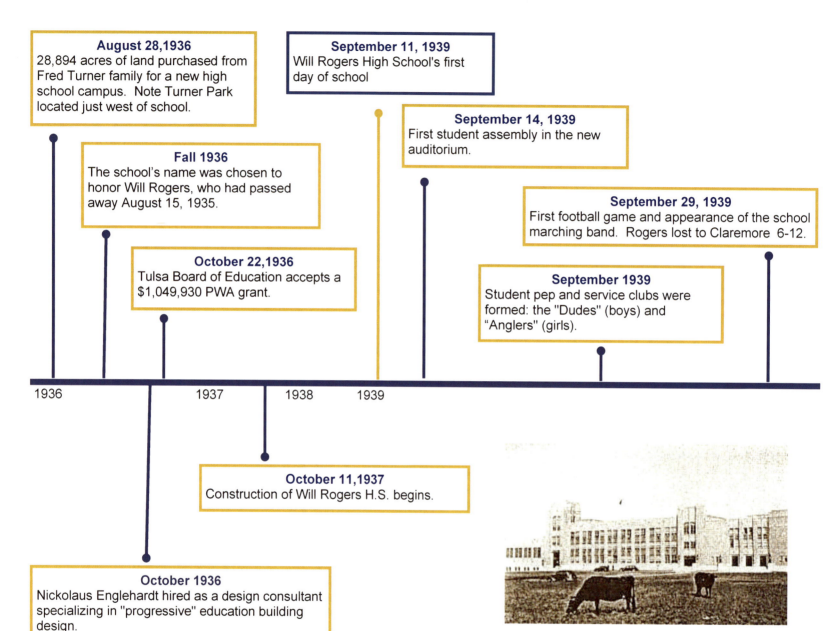

Picture from 1949 'Lariat' (circa 1939)

October, 1939
First football victory 14-6 over Broken Arrow High School.

1940
1st Faculty talent assembly.

Initial "Lariat" (school yearbook) is published.

November 3, 1939
Students & Faculty dedication of school.

November 4, 1939
School Celebration Will Rogers' Birthday.

Education Panels Over East Tower Doorway

1939 | 1940

November 5, 1939
Public open house/dedication attended by 10,000 (approximate Tulsa population 142,000).

March 7-8, 1940
First "Round Up" (school musical review)

April 5, 1940
North Central Association of Secondary Schools and Colleges grants Will Rogers High School accreditation.

February 1940
Application was made to North Central Association of Secondary Schools and Colleges for Accreditation.

May 1940
Initial Graduation commencement held for 329 students.

Will Rogers High School 1948 from the Beryl Ford Collection

1942 - 1946 World War II

World War II effected the high school in many ways. Gasoline rationing forced students to use school buses and bicycles for transportation to school. Many teachers joined the armed services or went to work in industries supporting the war. Students collected and donated scrap metal, supplies and materials for our soldiers.

December 1, 1944
The school was awarded the "Schools at War Flag" for raising war funds by selling significant amounts of war stamps.

1946 & 1947
74 World War II veterans enrolled to complete their high school degrees.

February 1943
Dancing was allowed for the first time on school property.

1945
Will Rogers won its 1st state football championship.

Timeline: 1941 | 1942 | 1943 | 1944 | 1945 | 1946 | 1947

Spring 1941
Basketball team wins the school's first state championship with a record of 18-4.

May 1943
The "Senior Breakfast" was cancelled because of food and gasoline rationing.

April 1942
"Time" and "Life" magazines feature articles about Will Rogers High School as an example of a "progressive education program."

1941 Class Assembly (Life Magazine)

Notice the Nazi like "flag salute" being made by the students reciting the Pledge of Allegiance.

This salute proposed by Francis Bellamy, author of the pledge, was replaced by the hand over the heart by an act of congress in 1942.

8

December 1952
Hawks-Terrell photographers make over 40 sepia enlargements of Will Rogers photographs provided by Claremore's Will Rogers Memorial Commission.

1950
Dr. Raymond Knight hired as principal. He served from 1950-1969

1948 | 1949 | 1950 | 1951 | 1952

December 1948
Football practice field is dedicated to Henry Franka Jr., who lost his life from a football game injury in 1946.

Spring 1948
Bob Canfield composes the words and music to W.R.H.S. Alma Mater

Spring 1948
Campus landscaping resumes. It was interrupted during the war.

April 1949
The class of 1947, donates a bust of Will Rogers, now located in the west foyer.

September 1949
The north east building expansion creates 8 new classrooms on two floors.

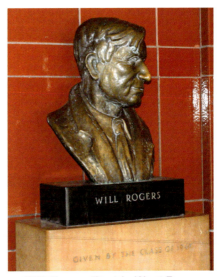

Will Rogers Bust in West Foyer

Timeline 1953–1960

1953
To ease classroom crowding pre-fab buildings were constructed on the north west side of the school.

January 1954
The Tamburinni portrait of Will Rogers was donated to the school by Sylvan N. Goldman.

1955-1956
Will Rogers were State Champions in football, basketball and cross country.

November 4, 1955
The parents of Oras Shaw (class of 1942) donated as a memorial to their son, the 1st electronic organ in Oklahoma.

October 11, 1957
Will Rogers High School was presented the prestigious Francis Bellamy Flag Award.

"The award, a large American flag, is given each year to an honored school of one of the forty-eight states. The school is selected on the basis of the outstanding achievements of the alumni, the citizenship and patriotism taught and practiced within the school, and the leadership displayed by the principal. The purpose of the award is to stimulate patriotism in the schools and to create a firm foundation for good citizenship. Will Rogers High School represented Oklahoma for the next fifty years as holder of this grand honor."
… 1958 *Lariat*

1958
School won its first State Wrestling Championship.

1960
State Football Championship

Shaw Memorial Organ

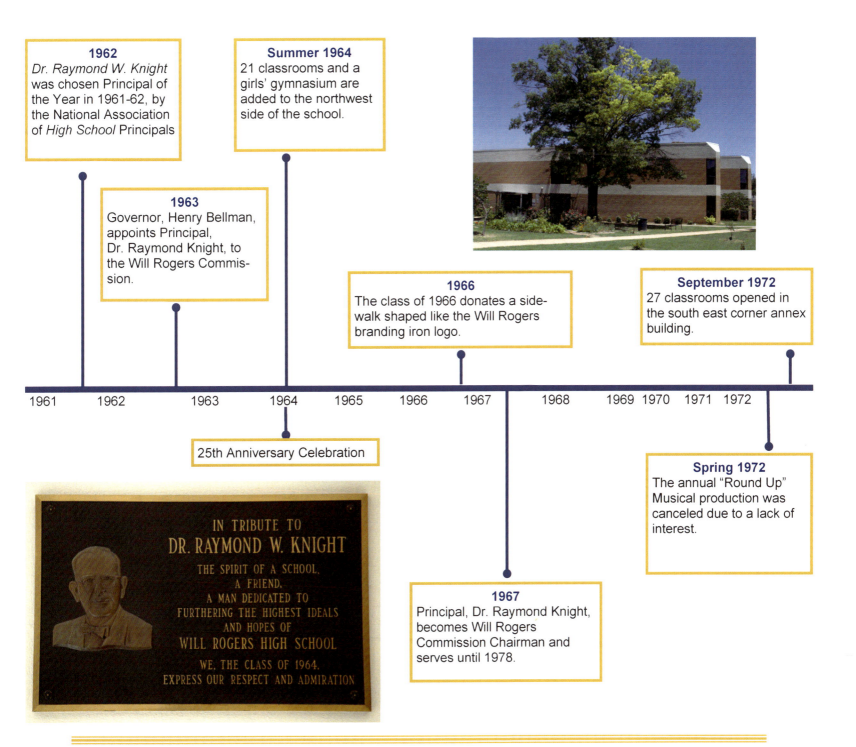

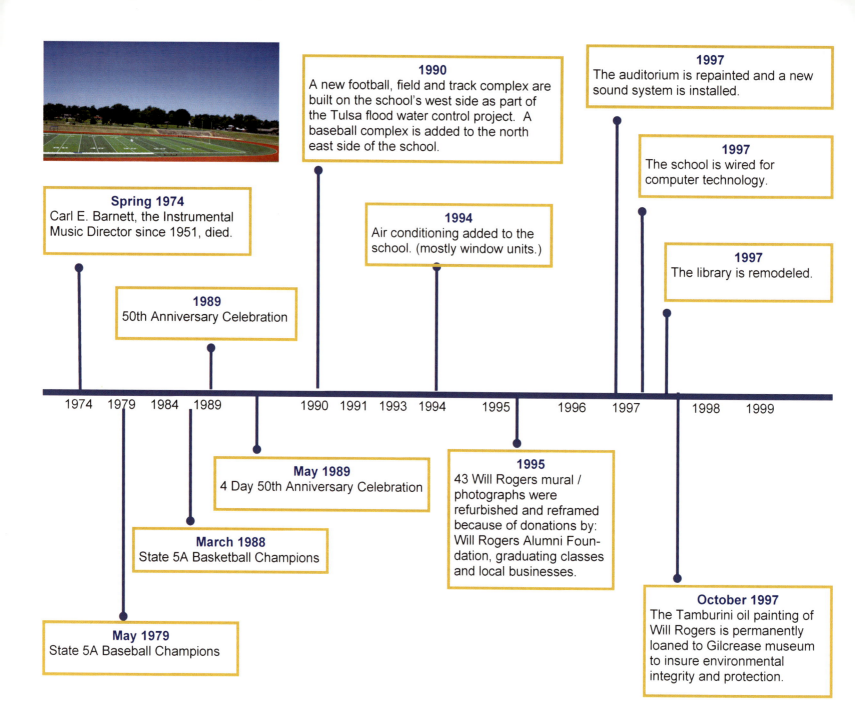

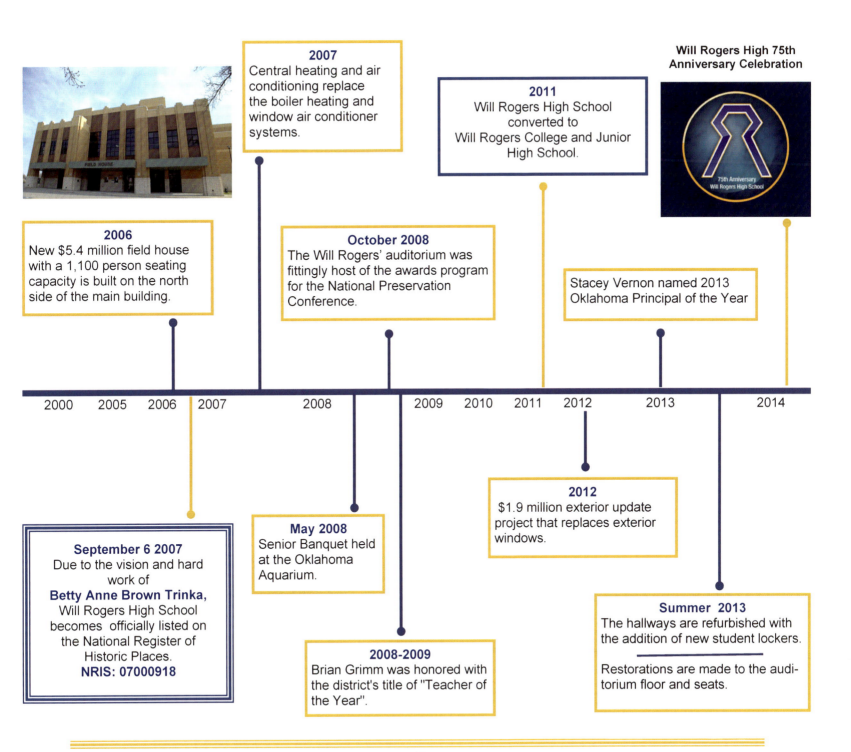

The Beginnings

In the mid-1930's, the Tulsa Public Schools were severely overcrowded. There were three high schools Booker T. Washington, Clinton High School, west of the river, and Central High School. Central had over 5000 students and was very crowded. The Tulsa Public School Board decided to build two high schools, one east of downtown and one on the west side of the Arkansas River. The two schools were originally named East Side (Will Rogers) and West Side (Daniel Webster).

Selecting a Location
The Tulsa Public School Board wanted the school location to coincide with the predicted growth of the city. An adequate transportation infrastructure was required to transport students to and from school. In the 1930's, the most prominent road through Tulsa was Route 66, which travels down 11th street.

Another consideration was to locate the school in a position of anticipated population growth. The location of the University of Tulsa, just to the west of Harvard was a good indicator that the city would grow east of its campus.

Building a Progressive School
One of the popular trends of the time was to provide what was termed a "progressive" education. At that time education policy was very structured. Every student got only the education they required for an elected career. The majority would receive vocational training and only a minority would receive an academic education. Progressive education focused on a core education for all with much more emphasis on artistic and creative endeavors.

To assure the new school was designed to accommodate this new educational philosophy, the school board contracted a nationally recognized school planner, Nickolaus Louis Englehardt, to assist in developing a school design to implement a progressive school program.

Selecting a Name
On August 15, 1935, Will Rogers died in an airplane crash in Point Barrow, Alaska. This was an international tragedy. The Tulsa School Board renamed "East Side" to "Will Rogers High School" in honor of the recently deceased superstar.

On August 28, 1936 the school board purchased 26.9 acres of farm land situated east of the University of Tulsa for the high school campus. The land was purchased from the Fred Turner family for $21,772. The city park just west of the school is named for Fred Turner.

On October 22, 1936 the Tulsa Board of Education accepted a $1,049,930 Public Works Administration (PWA) grant to fund approximately 40% of the schools' construction. This led to the art deco style of the school being classified as a PWA style of art deco. Unlike mot PWA style buildings, Will Rogers is quite lavish and more like a decorative office building.

Will Rogers East Tower and Entrance

The Architects

A. M. Atkinson

Shortly after funding the Will Rogers High School project, the Tulsa School Board assigned A. M. Atkinson to be the manager of the project. He was given the title of "Supervising Architect." One of his first responsibilities was to select and hire the architects to build the school.

After deliberation he chose Leon Senter and Joseph Koberling as architects to design the building. Koberling had the creative artistic talents and Senter had the construction management skills, experience and reputation.

From that point on, Atkinson functioned as liaison between the architects and school board assuring the paperwork to support the construction project was kept up to date and alleviating unnecessary distractions by the school board during construction.

Leon Senter

Leon Senter, regarded as the Dean of Oklahoma Architects, was issued License # 1 in 1929, when licensing became a state requirement. Senter was the President of the Oklahoma State Board of Governors of Licensed Architects and a charter member and president of the Tulsa Oklahoma Chapter of AIA.

Senter had a proven record of being able to manage large projects. He was chief architect for the following Tulsa buildings prior to the Will Rogers High School project: The Tulsa Coliseum, Philcade, Skelly Stadium (1930), Tulsa Fire Alarm Building, Tulsa Municipal Airport Terminal (1932) and Union Bus Depot(1935).

Joseph Koberling Jr.

Joseph Koberling Jr. was born in Budapest Hungary in 1900 and earned his B.A. in Architecture in 1925 from the Armour Institute of Chicago, Illinois. He was the son of the architect of Tulsa's "Cave House" on Charles Page Blvd.

Koberling was a previous associate of A. M. Atkinson, who was assigned to elect the managing architects of the school construction project. They had worked together as architects of the Public Service Company Building and Tulsa Medical Arts Building.

"We felt it should be a worthy tribute and memorial to a man everyone loved so well. It seemed to us that the building should be monumental in character. However because it was a school it should not be a somber type of monumental memorial. Rather it should be alive and joyous in character, not only reflecting his own outlook on life but the spirit and aspiration of the generation of young men and women who were to use the structure as a place of learning and training to become useful citizens throughout the coming years.

The vertical lines, the massing of the entrances, the ornamentation, and the selection of materials and colors through out the project were deliberately studied to produce this desired effect."
  Architect Joseph Koberling: on Will Rogers High School

The School's Design

The exterior of the building has a strong horizontal presence that spans nearly two blocks east-west. This horizontal orientation is balanced by a vertical emphasis typical of the zigzag style of art deco architecture.

The artistic value of Will Rogers High School's interior was a collaboration of artisans' contracted by Koberling and Senter.

Alex C. Rindskoph, a nationally known interior decorator Is responsible for many of the most artistic and creative features in the building. He designed the entry porticos, library and the interior decorations of the Auditorium. He also painted the auditorium mural.

Karl Kolstad and John Sand, Jr. were artistic craftsmen, taking Koberling sketches and turning them into finished terra-cotta art deco units. The architects beautifully integrated the modern architecture of the day with quality materials and first-class craftsmanship.

Built: 1938
Style: PWA Art Deco
Address: 3909 E. 5th Place

Architects: Joseph R. Koberling
Leon B. Senter
A. M. Atkinson

Artists: Joseph R. Koberling
Alex C. Rindskoph
Karl Kolstad
John Sand, Jr.

Consultant: Nickolaus Louis Englehardt

NRIS: 07000918

Stairwell in the East Foyer

School Construction

The architects carefully designed 101 building features to create an efficient education facility including a modern architecture style with artistic features. This was accomplished with high quality materials and craftsmanship.

The school was built atop a hill that initially made the school visible from downtown Tulsa. The school became known as "Will on the Hill." The building faces south with a split level design that utilizes the natural east to west slope of the hill.

The school has a limestone foundation on the basement level topped by brick walls. There are four floors of classrooms and offices. Two large towers provide entry to the school that contain stairwells for access to the upper floors of the building. As you enter the south doors, you are actually on the second floor of the building.

The original 1939 building provided 200,000 square feet of classroom and office space.

An aerial view of the construction of Will Rogers High School, May 1938. The gymnasium, auditorium, and cafeteria exteriors were still under construction. Notice the lack of homes surrounding the school. (Beryl Ford Collection).

Details Make a Masterpiece

Finials - an architectural decorative device used at the top, end, or corner of a structure

Capital - the topmost member of a column

Apron - a raised section of ornamental stonework below a window ledge or roof line, typically stone tablet, or monument

Parapet - a low wall projecting from the edge of a platform, terrace or roof

Pilaster - a slightly projecting column built into or applied to the face of a wall

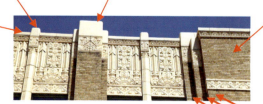

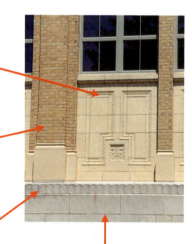

Stepped Pilasters

Fluted Belt

Inset - something smaller inserted into something larger

Bedford Limestone - Also known as Indiana limestone

Terra Cotta - fired clay used especially for statuettes and other architectural design purposes

Through the book terms unfamiliar to the general public are used. Some of those terms are defined for better understanding.

Entry from West Vestibule

Main Hallway

Terrazzo Floors - with an art deco designed boarder

Terrazzo - a ground and polished surface appearing smooth, producing an uniformly textured surface

Foyer - an entrance hall or other open area in a building.

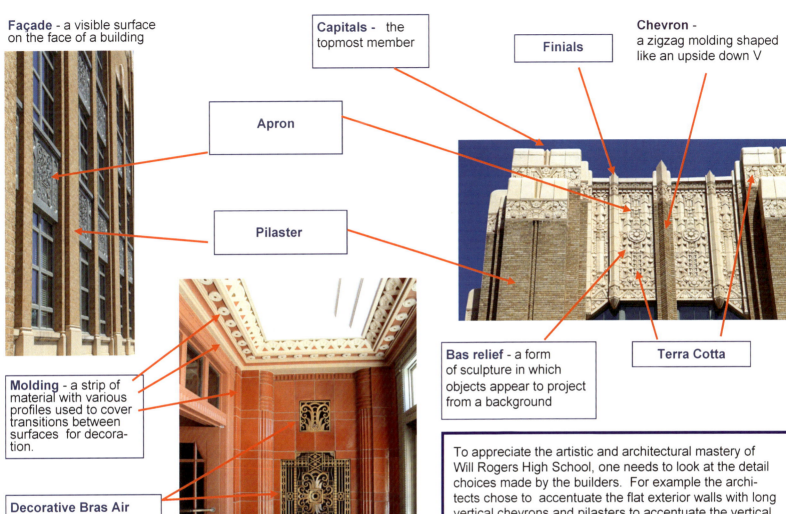

Façade - a visible surface on the face of a building

Capitals - the topmost member

Finials

Chevron - a zigzag molding shaped like an upside down V

Apron

Pilaster

Bas relief - a form of sculpture in which objects appear to project from a background

Terra Cotta

Molding - a strip of material with various profiles used to cover transitions between surfaces for decoration.

Decorative Bras Air Vents - in an art deco floral design

Interior entrance to foyer

Vestibule - a lobby, entrance hall, or passage between the entrance and the interior of a building

To appreciate the artistic and architectural mastery of Will Rogers High School, one needs to look at the detail choices made by the builders. For example the architects chose to accentuate the flat exterior walls with long vertical chevrons and pilasters to accentuate the vertical nature of a horizontally oriented building.

In the interior they replaced plain painted walls with more expensive red terra cotta tiles with gold leaf accents and curved corners. They installed terrazzo floors with art deco boarder designs. Appreciate the wide decorative ceiling molding and decorative brass air vents.

The building is truly extraordinary in the combination of art and form. One just has to take the time to stop and appreciate the fine details.

19

School Opens

Will Rogers High School was officially opened for school on September 14, 1939. There were 44 teachers and administrators for 1501 students. They held their first assembly and began creating groups to coordinate the development of school institutions and standards. They needed to elect class officers and create a student government. They organized groups to decide on such things as school colors and a nickname.

Students had many surprises when school began. For one thing it was out in the middle of nowhere surrounded by pasture land and grazing cattle. As students entered the main entrance, they discovered an elegant foyer that was more like an expensive office building than a public school. The floors were polished terrazzo and the walls were gleaming mandarin red terra cotta rather than painted plaster. The doors were inset and framed in terra cotta with painted gold leaf patterns.

No school in the state was as luxurious as Will Rogers. The school was designed to support the progressive curriculum being developed by Tulsa Public Schools under the guidance of consultant Nickolaus Louis Englehardt. Classrooms were painted colors selected to coincide with the temperament of the class subject material being presented. Five different color schemes were used for classrooms. Mathematics and science classes used bright energetic colors where more subdued pastels were used in the library.

The students of Will Rogers were the first students to benefit from the national progressive education movement. This meant that the education the student received would be experience driven rather than content driven. Students were encouraged to be independent thinkers rather than memorizing a plethora of unconnected facts. They were taught how to think for themselves rather than what to think.

School Symbolism

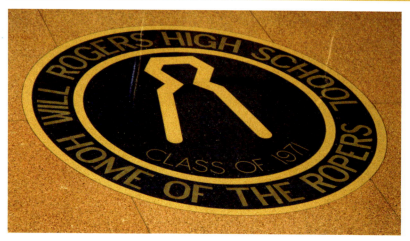

Inlaid in the terrazzo floor of the west foyer is the Will Rogers High School logo donated to the school by the Class of 71

School Name - Will Rogers High School

Shortly after the death of Will Rogers, the Tulsa School board re-named Eastside High School to Will Rogers High School. It was the first school in the country to be named after Rogers.

School Colors
Royal Blue & Gold

Community popular name:

"Will on the Hill."

School Logo - Interpretation of Branding Iron

The most iconic symbol of Will Rogers is the unique artistic interpretation of the Rogers ranch's branding iron. Shown to the left, this symbol is found through out the school. It is also imprinted on senior class rings and is the definitive school logo.

Will Rogers Dog Iron (branding iron) Found at Will's Ranch and Birthplace Home in Oologah Oklahoma

Victory Song
March down the field
To victory for our school.
We will always be true
To the Gold and Blue
Showing loyalty to you
Rah! Rah!
We give the best
That we possess to our school
So here's a toast
To the school we boast
To our own Will Rogers High!

Ride on Ropers
Ride on your Ropers, ride on to your fame.
There's no foe can daunt you
for your bear Will Rogers name.
Rah Rah Rah
Rope 'em and brand 'em
Lead 'em to corral.
Round up those wandering doggies,
Central's grazing in hostile locale.

22

School Nickname - Ropers

When the school opened, a student committee was formed to choose a school nickname. A local beer manufacture, Ahrens Brewery, had a popular beer named "Ranger Beer." The Brewery offered each of the boys in the school a free jacket with the Ranger Beer logo if they chose "Rogers Rangers" as the school nickname.

The school administrators nixed the students' plans and the "Rogers Rangers" became the "Rogers Ropers." Ahrens Brewing Company went bankrupt in February 1940.

School Alma Mater

The alma mater was written in 1948 by a student in the senior class. Bob Canfield composed both the words and music to the Alma Mater.

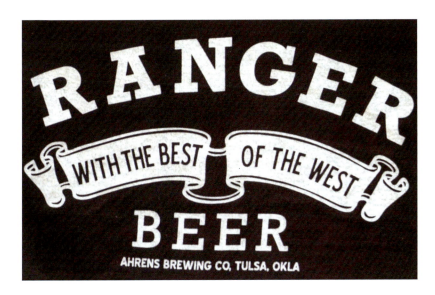

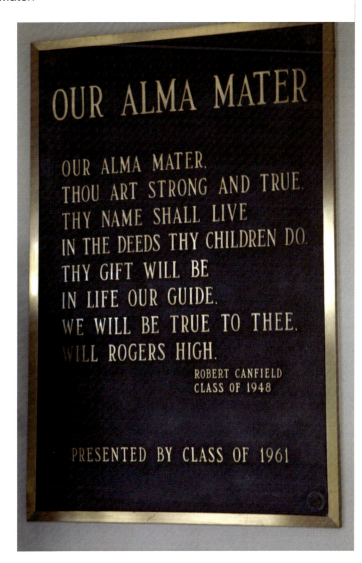

Alma Mater Plaque located in the Main Hall

Yearbook - Lariat
The annual yearbook, the "Lariat", provides a time capsule of our time at Will Rogers. It provides a chronicle of who we were, who we knew and what we did in those brief years in high school.

23

Student Life

Students at Will Rogers High School have created a legacy rich with tradition. Many remnants of this legacy are found on the campus grounds and in the halls of the school.

Will Rogers students are taught to respect the school and the students who came before them. They are encouraged, but not required, to leave their mark for future generations of school students.

After 75 years of student donations, the school halls are decked with plaques commemorating veterans, students, faculty and donors to the school and its students.

Will Rogers Bust

Located in the west foyer on a marble pedestal, is a bronze bust of Will Rogers. Notice the highly decorative mandarin red terracotta inset with gold leaf trimming.

For years students passing the statue, would rub the statue for good luck.

The statue was a senior class gift by the Class of 1945.

Senior Bench

The "Senior Bench" was the initial senior class gift given by the Class of 1940. In front of the bench, etched in concrete, are the names of the 329 initial Will Rogers graduates. The bench is dedicated to Clarence Jones, a member of the class, who lost his life in an automobile accident in 1939. He created the modified dog-iron design of the Will Rogers' logo for the senior rings.

The Tamburini Portrait

The only painting for which Will Rogers ever posed was painted by Italian artist, Arnaldo Tamburini. Will's wife, Betty, was responsible for convincing Will to pose for the portrait just one month before his fatal aircraft crash in Alaska.

In 1954 Sylvian M. Goldman, a friend of the Rogers' family, bought and donated the painting to Will Rogers High School. The painting was displayed at the school from 1954 - 1997. In 1997, the painting was permanently loaned to Gilcrease Museum, because of environmental and security concerns.

Roper Path

Located on the south lawn is a unique walking path in the shape of the Will Rogers High School's (branding iron) Logo. This path was a gift of the class of 1966

Roper of the Month

There is a monthly award that results in a premium parking spot on the south side oval.

Class Pranks

Each year it is a tradition that senior students are expected to commit a "senior prank". These unorganized practical jokes live on as legends passed from class to class.

Stealing Central Spirit
One year during football season, before the big rival game with Central, the large brass statue "The Great Spirit" was taken from the Central High School lobby and mysteriously appeared in Will Rogers' north parking lot. When Central High School was relocated, the statue was moved to the west side of Woodward Park.

Alligator in the Hall
One year, as the legend goes, an alligator was borrowed from the Tulsa Zoo and appeared in the school's main hallway. It was lassoed in true roper fashion and dragged into the teachers' lounge.

Student Organizations

Extra curricular activities are an important factor in the development of the whole student. Clubs and student activities round out the social development of the student.

The Will Rogers College and High School website references the following organizations:

- Student Council
- Book Club
- Chess Club
- Fine Arts
    - Band
    - Drama
    - Orchestra
    - Visual Arts
- Athletics
    - Basketball (Boys and Girls)
    - Cheerleading
    - Cross Country (Boys and Girls)
    - Fast Pitch Softball (Boys and Girls)
    - Football (High School and Junior High)
    - Golf (Boys and Girls)
    - Power Lifting
    - Soccer (Boys and Girls)
    - Swimming
    - Tennis
    - Girls Track

Electronic Age

The age of electronics has forever changed the way students communicate and learn. Students can optionally join a network called "Celly" and receive notifications and updates via text messages to their cell phone. They can also use the texting system to make inquiries and communicate with teachers and school administrators.

Instrumental Music

The instrumental music department plays a key role in many school activities. The marching band practices as many hours as the football team to support the team spirit from the stands to present half time shows.

**Will Rogers Marching Band
from the Beryl Ford Collection**

There are a number of bands including the marching band, stage band, orchestra and special bands to support "Round Up" and other school productions.

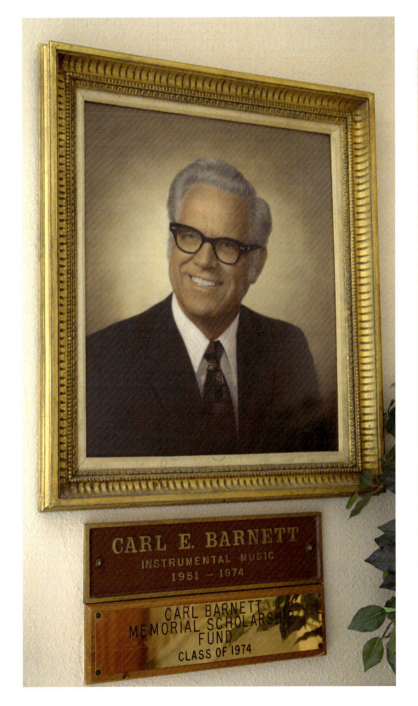

Carl E. Barnett

This author has very fond memories of Mr. Barnett. He appeared to get great pleasure from giving me a hard time. He used to constantly tell me "You're no musician, you're a drummer." He always did it in fun with no malice. The first year at Rogers I didn't make the marching band. He had plenty of drummers and I couldn't play anything else. He was right, I was just a drummer.

That year in band class, I met the lady who was to become the mother of my four children. She made the marching band and I would attend every game and sit on the border between the students and the band. I was kind of a pest and by the second year Mr. Barnett put me in the marching band with out even a trial. He told me " I might as well put you in the band, you're going to be there bothering me anyway."

He was a great organizer and band leader. We had a fund raiser each year where the students sold "Texas Manor" fruit cakes. They were good, unlike the store-bought cakes.

His bands always had first-class equipment. We didn't take wasteful trips to exotic locations like Disney World or the big holiday parades. He invested in durable equipment, sheet music and musical instruments. If a student needed an instrument, they could check one out from the band instrument locker. He purchased numerous specialty instruments that even the Tulsa Philharmonic didn't have. They would borrow unique instruments from us quite often.

Don Wagner

Carl Barnett died of a heart attack on April 23,1974 during a performance on the Will Rogers auditorium stage conducting a performance of Bach's "Come Sweet Death." Students staying late for activities in the auditorium and janitors have reported seeing his ghost lurking around the stage.

Student Athletics

1965 Lariat

Will Rogers State Championships

Football
- 1956
- 1957
- 1960
- 1961

Baseball
- 1968
- 1973
- 1978
- 1979

Basketball
- 1941
- 1956
- 1958
- 1988
- 1996

Wrestling
- 1956

Cross Country
- 1947
- 1948
- 1956
- 1957
- 1995

Track & Field
- 1943
- 1944
- 1945
- 1947
- 1948
- 1949

Golf
- 1980

Swimming
- 1958

Will Rogers has a rich athletic tradition. Over the 75 year history of the school, it has achieved numerous distinctions. Sporting events were community events involving more than just the athletes. There were cheerleaders, marching band and pep squad members, as well as parents and other school patrons at games.

FOUNDERS
Johnnie Egbert '65
Art Fleak '65
Vic Prather '65
Gloria Mitchell Roling '65
Larry Skelton '65
Norman Summers '65
Butch Watson '65

CHARTER MEMBERS
Teddy Aguilar '66
Tony Bacher '66
Bill Barnes '72
Mahala Baxter '66
Robert Baxter
Ernie Bedford '65
Larry M. Brown '49
Bob Bryant '65
Sharon Stafford Bynum '60
Steve Chesebro '59
Gil Cloud '64
Frances Hawpe Compton '64
Debbie Fleak Crissup '69
Ronald Crow '66
Coach Art Davis
Johnnie Egbert '65
Susan B. Evans
Jim Ferris '67
Art Fleak '65
Diane Moore Gearhart '65
Bill Geier '66
Paul George '66
Joey Grayson '66
Karen DeMonte Isley '65
Janie Moore Joswick '62
Mr. and Mrs. Larry Kelley '70
Susan Ryals Kelley '70
Gary Llewellyn '65
Jack London '60
Marvin Mann
Beverly Marquardt '66
Mike Marrs '64
Sherryl Mellott McGuire '65
Don Mellott '62
Steve Montgomery '67
Vic Prather '65
Bill Prather '66
Tim Raburn
David Rader '75
Ken Ragan '66
Gloria Mitchell Roling '65
Dave Sanders '65
Steve Sanders
Pat Pollard Schroeder '45
Larry Skelton '65
Bob Smith '63
Al St. John '59
Iris Warlick Studenny '66
Norman Summers '65
Tom Trimble '64
John Turner '61
John Ward '66
Butch Watson '65
Jan Davies Weinheimer '66
Dick Welch '49
Linda Smith White '64
Rick White '66
Robert Williams '65
Dennis Wilson '66
Ron Woods '57
Jim Young '49

The mission of the Will Rogers High School All-Sports Booster Club is:

to support the sports with the needs that can't be provided by the District and school.

to build pride in the programs and create memorable experiences for the athletes.

to continue the tradition and legacy in the new Will Rogers College High.

Contact the school to learn how you can become involved.

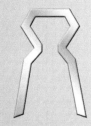

Ride on ye Ropers!
Ride on to your fame.
There's no foe can daunt you
for you bear Will Rogers' name.
Rah Rah Rah
Rope 'em and brand 'em
Lead 'em to corral.
Round up those wanderin' doggies,
Central's grazin' in hostile locale.

The Round Up

The "Round-Up" is the annual musical review that features multiple musical productions. It is created through a collaboration of students, teachers, parents and alumni. The group performs all the tasks required for putting on a Broadway production including:

- Raising production funds
- Devising a theme
- Designing and building stage sets
- Designing and sewing costumes
- Music selection and arrangement
- Choreography
- Promotion and ticket sales

The "Round Up" was presented annually from 1940 through 1971. It was not produced between 1972 and 1995 due to a lack of interests by faculty and students. Since then it has become a popular event, and is presented each Spring.

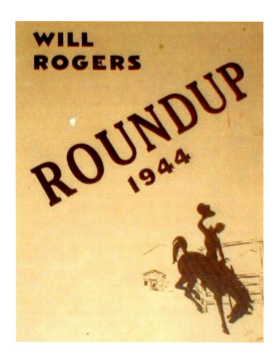

The Lariat

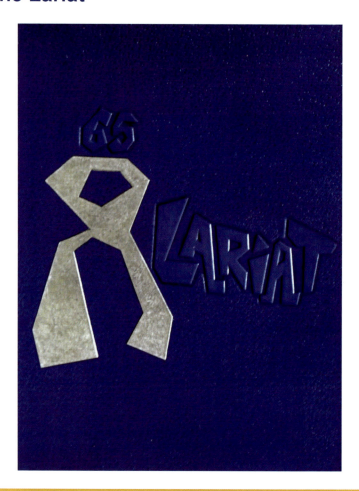

I recently reviewed the year book from my senior year (1965) and found a version of myself that I had forgotten existed. I wouldn't have even recognized my own picture had it not been labeled. But for some odd reason old friends looked just the way I remembered them. Heart warming memories came from the words written by friends in the back of the book. I wonder what I wrote in their books.

Don Wagner

Dr. Raymond W. Knight

Dr. Raymond W. Knight was principal from 1950 through 1969. During that time he distinguished himself as an educator, administrator and guardian of Will Rogers' heritage.

In 1963, Dr. Knight was presented the "Principal of the Year" award for the 1961 - 1962 school year by the National Association of High School Principals. That same year he was appointed by Governor Henry Bellman to the Will Rogers Commission which oversees the museum and birthplace of Rogers.

Dr. Knight served as the chairman of the commission from 1967 - 1978. An annual scholarship is given each year to a Will Rogers' graduate in his name.

Portrait of Dr. Raymond Knight hanging in Main Hall

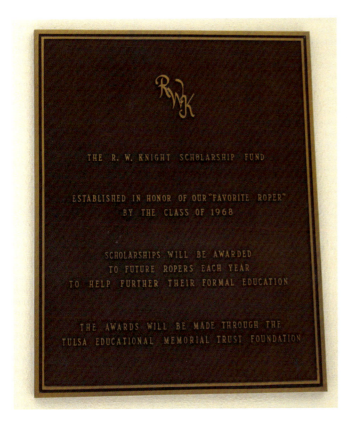

Plaque commemorating RWK Scholarship in Auditorium Foyer

"We were so inspired by Dr. Raymond Knight, who was our principal. He instilled in us a reverence for the facility. We were brought up to believe it was something to be taken care of."

, Betty Ann (Brown) Trinka
From Tulsa World Interview

Patriotism & Veterans Memorials

Will Rogers' students and faculty have always displayed their admiration and respect for those who have served our country. Several plaques are found throughout the school that have been donated to honor those veterans. Look at the plaque on the left and all of those Will Rogers' students that gave their lives in service to our country.

World War II Memorial Plaque in Main Hall

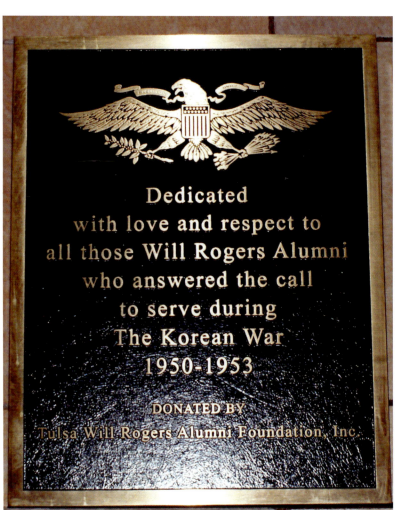

Korean War Memorial Plaque in Main Hall

Vietnam War Memorial Plaque in Main Hall

October 11, 1957
Will Rogers was presented the prestigious
Francis Bellamy Flag Award

Francis Bellamy (1855-1931), a Baptist Minister, wrote the original Pledge of Allegiance in 1892. It was first published in the Sept. 8, 1892, edition of "The Youth's Companion Magazine", which Bellamy was editor. He composed the pledge for school children to commemorate the 400th anniversary of Columbus' discovery of America.

Each year the Rome, New York (Bellamy's home town) Elks Lodge selects a school to receive the "Francis Bellamy Flag Award" for leadership and patriotism. Only one award is given annually. Each state has one recipient who holds the award for 50 years.

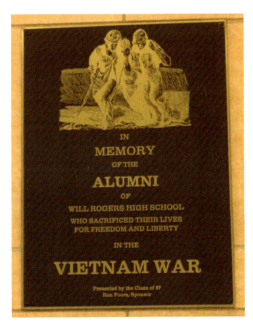

Veteran Honorarium Plaque in Main Hall

American Creed in Auditorium Foyer

Will Rogers Photo Collection

In the halls at Rogers High School, hangs a remarkable collection of framed photographs and portraits of Will Rogers and associates. The majority of the collection is located along the east hallway, adjacent to the auditorium.

The pictures cover a variety of very popular people of his time and the various aspects of his career.

Some of the people pictured include:

Charles Lindbergh	Noah Berry
Amelia Earhart	Irvin S. Cobb
Henry Ford	John D. Rockefeller
Edsel Ford	Robert Russell Moton
Charles Short	Wiley Post
Shirley Temple	

Will with Shirley Temple

Will with Charles Lindberg

Will with Irene Rich from "The Cowboy and the Lady"

Introduction to Art Deco

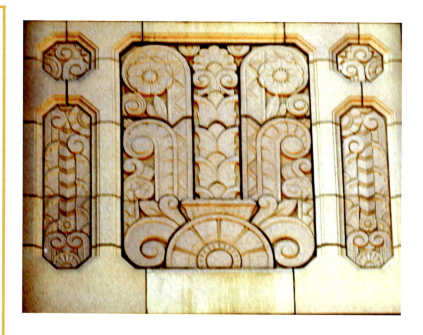

History of Art Deco
In 1925, at the "Le Musee des Arts Decoratifs", art exposition, the term "Art Deco" was first used to define a category of Modernism Art. The U.S. Secretary of Commerce, Herbert Hoover, sent art and architecture experts to learn and adapt these new designs into American architecture. These and other American attendees utilized the decorative architectural design that became known as "Art Deco". Art Deco consists of all forms of decorative expression. This includes furniture, flatware, fixtures, art and interior designs.

Art Deco Styles
Art Deco is a design of ornamentation and geometry merged with color, texture and light. There are three primary styles of Art Deco: Zigzag, Streamline and the Depression or PWA (Public Works Administration) style. The Zigzag and Streamline styles are very distinct and are represented by differentiating form and features. The Depression style is more historically defined by the time of construction and means of funding. It takes on the features and characteristics of zigzag or streamline forms of art deco.

The time period most commonly associated with Art Deco Architecture is from 1925 to 1941, although the same design features of that period are still being utilized in current building designs.

PWA / Depression Style
The "PWA/Depression" style of architecture was funded partially with public money in a period that included recovery from the Great Depression. The Fair Grounds Pavilion, Tulsa Union Depot, Daniel Webster High School and Will Rogers High School are examples of this style.

Zigzag Style
Most of the Tulsa Art Deco is of the "Zigzag" style that emphasizes strong vertical lines and angular geometric patterns. Tulsa examples of this style include Boston Avenue Methodist Church, Farmers Market, Oklahoma Natural Gas and the Philcade building.

Streamline Style
The "Streamline" style is more horizontally oriented and typically features aerodynamic flowing curves. Tulsa examples of this style include The Brook Restaurant, City Veterinary and the Day & Nite Cleaners.

Metro Deco
A deco style commonly used in metropolitan cities that incorporates the angular geometric zigzag patterns, but is more horizontal than vertical is commonly referred to as "Metro Deco."

Retro Deco
Today the art deco principles are still being applied to building designs. These building are commonly categorized as "Retro Deco" designs.

Art Deco of Will Rogers

Will Rogers High School is an extraordinary architecturally designed building The school was built with 40% WPA funds and is therefore classified as an Art Deco WPA style of building. The WPA grant allowed the builders to use materials and craftsmen that would not have been affordable for typical school buildings. As a result, artists and craftsmen were used in place of typical construction workers on many phases of this construction project. The architects did a remarkable job of realizing what they could accomplish with this talent and created beautiful and intricate designs for these craftsmen to implement.

Look at how complicated the corner of the tower (shown to the left) was designed. The long vertical sections are called pilasters. They protrude and highlight the vertical direction of a column. These are not ordinary pilasters. They are layered atop each other on both sides of the corner column. This stepped series of pilasters accentuate the vertical nature of the towers.   Notice that in the center of the outmost pilasters is a vertical line created by two reverse chevrons ("W" shape) that runs from the base of the tower to the top.

Corner of the South-West Tower

The pilasters are topped by terra cotta capitals with decorative floral aprons. The capitals have curved corners and continue the reverse chevron patterns of the pilasters.

Exterior Designs

Will Rogers High School is a split level design with three floors and a basement. It is situated on a hill sloping from east to west and exposes differential portions of the first floor depending on your location. The building has a Bedford limestone basement that is topped by three floors of gold brick walls. A narrow limestone fluted belt serves as the junction between the limestone basement and the brick walls.

Two nearly symmetrical bay towers on each side of the main hallway are the central focal points of the building's south façade and provide entrance to the school. The tower encases a stairwell that connects four floors of classrooms. On the west corner of the building is the gymnasium with locker rooms beneath.

Between the two towers are classrooms and offices. The upper two floors contain classrooms. The main hall connecting the two towers includes the library and the school's primary offices. The south east corner of the building contains the school auditorium with three doors opening to a foyer.

The east tower/entrance to the school was designed as the secondary entrance, but today for security reasons, is the primary visitors entrance. The east tower is designed similar to the west tower. Due to elevation differences, the east tower is shorter to create a level appearance between the towers.

West Tower Entrance

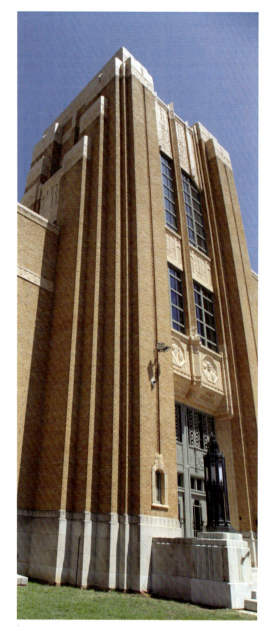

The most eye-catching focal point of the school is the west entrance and tower that is situated between the gymnasium and the main hallway that includes the school offices and library. Bedford limestone stairs, porch and side walls frame access to elaborate art deco styled entry doors to the school's main foyer.

The tower has alternating sections of terra cotta and windows that provide natural light in the stairways. The metal entry doors have a distinctive zigzag deco appearance.

In the corners of the porch are narrow stand alone lanterns on fluted limestone pedestals. The black metal lanterns have a cupola style with an open base crowned with a light and a decorative pinnacle.

Gymnasium & West Exterior

The west face of the building is the west side of the gymnasium, locker rooms and swimming pool. Due to elevation differences much more of the Bedford limestone base is displayed. A fluted limestone belt separates the first and second floors of the building. The design of the south side of the building is extended to the west with vertical emphasis of stepped columns and layered pilasters.

Office / Library / Classrooms

The section of the building between the two towers, on the entry level, houses the library and school administration offices. The basement and upper two floors accommodate classrooms.

The façade of this section is a repeating sequence of vertical, two step pilasters that extend from the basement to the roof of the building. The pilasters encase two sets of windows on each floor divided by a single step pilaster that extends from the basement to just above the top window ledge. This creates eight identical bays between the towers. Three floors of windows are separated by two gray-green terracotta aprons with a floral-stem design. Although the south façade is nearly two blocks long, the design features emphasize the verticality of the school.

East Tower & Entrance

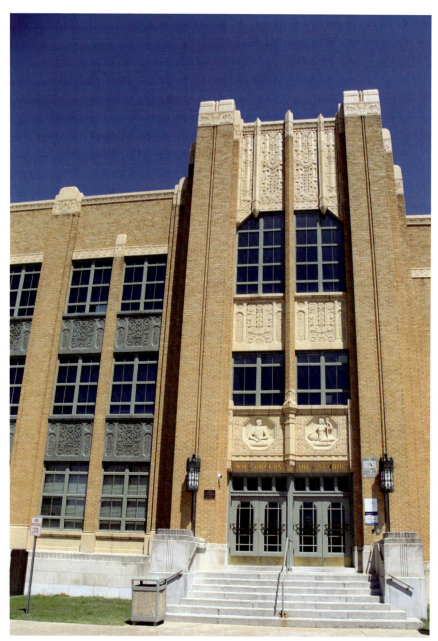

A three story tower with long and narrow columns has duplicated the appearance of the west tower. Due to the building being built on a hill sloping east to west, the east tower is shorter and has fewer windows than the west tower. The tower again emphasizes verticality with stepped columns, chevron pilasters and upright insets on the columns. The columns of the tower are topped with terra cotta capitals identical to the west tower.

The exterior east tower appears similar to the west tower, except it displays the "Education" rather than the "Will Rogers" panels.

Hanging Lanterns

Lighting each entry is a pair of ornate lanterns. The doors on the east tower have wall sconces whereas the west entryway and auditorium entrances have free standing lanterns.

The artistic sconce design is an interpretive floral pattern that is different than the design of the free standing lanterns.

"V" shaped insets over the wall lanterns divide pilasters running from the top of the lanterns to the capital molding on the roof.

Auditorium Entrance

The style of the auditorium entry is complimentary yet, different to the east and west tower entrances It has three pairs of deco-styled doors that are identical to the tower entrances. Three distinct terra cotta panels serve as dividers between doors and windows. Narrow vertical terra cotta dividers begin above the doors, dividing the panels and bay windows. The door modules are separated by stepped pilasters emphasizing the vertical design of the building. Lighting is provided by two stand alone lanterns identical to those found at the west tower entrance.

Will Rogers & Education Panels

Will Rogers Panels

On the east and west tower hang a pair of bas relief terra cotta panels designed by architect Joseph Koberling.

Above the west doors the panels feature two periods of Will Rogers' life. The right panel depicts his cowboy days with a cowboy hat, horse and roped steer. The left panel is about his movie days with a movie reel camera, an airplane, and a polo rider. The octagon frames around the portraits are surrounded by cornucopia and floral design.

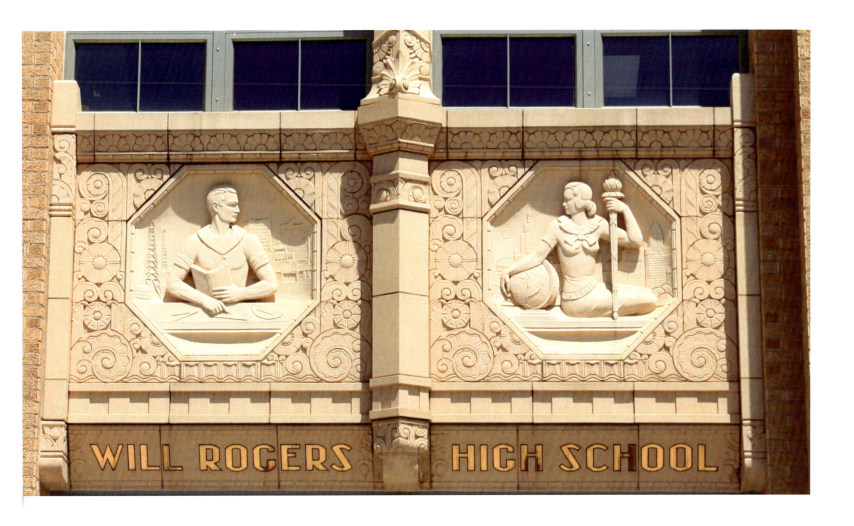

Education Panels

The sculptures on the east tower present a boy with elements such as a protractor, ruler and compass supporting a technical education. In his background are oil derricks, an airplane and Tulsa office buildings, that give homage to the business development of Tulsa. The right education panel displays a girl holding the torch of knowledge and a globe which represents the liberal arts aspects of education. In her background is the skyline of Tulsa displaying such landmarks as the Philtower, Exchange National Bank (now Bank of Oklahoma Building), and the Christian Science Church.

Art Deco Interior

The interior of the school is exquisite. The appearance of the public areas: tower entrance vestibules, foyer and main hall of the school are very unique and elaborate. The halls feature terrazzo floors with an art deco square pattern. A color scheme featuring Chinese mandarin red tiles with gold highlights and brass grills decorates the main public areas of the school.

Natural light from the front doors and tower windows supplement the Koberling designed art deco hanging lights. The hallway doorways are inset and feature art deco style archways. These doorways are often decorated with red terra cotta tiles with gold trimmed headers. It is common to find inset bays displaying pictures, plaques or statues.

Entering the School

West Tower Front Doors to Portico

Entering the school through the art-deco styled doors on the towers leads to a lavish portico. Notice all the beautiful artistic details and craftsmanship utilized in creating these entryways.

There are beautiful intricate brass air vents at each end of the portico. The vents are centered in a terra cotta tiled inset with curved fluted corners.

West Tower Portico

The doors to the building interior match the design of the exterior doors but are the mandarin-red color used in the portico and interior of the school. This provides a transition from the exterior blue-gray look to the red and gold interior motif.

The ceiling has wonderful multi-layered molding and uniquely designed art deco styled lights.

This is certainly one of the most ornate and unique entryways in Tulsa.

49

West Foyer & Tower Staircase

The west foyer is the most impressive entrance to the school. Wide terrazzo steps with brass rails lead to a lobby that provides entry to the gymnasium, classrooms and the main hallway connecting the two south towers. One enters the building on the second floor. Wide terrazzo stairwells located on each side of the entryway provide access to the upper floors through the tower. The stairs have a fluted, red terra cotta, top molding that blends at the base into a large rounded corner pedestal.

The foyer has terrazzo floors with an art deco square pattern with curved bends around the stairwell corners. As one ascends the stairwell, natural light shines though the decorative ironwork on the exterior tower façade. The foyer is illuminated by lights hanging from the ceiling. The doors to the gymnasium are inset and decorated above the door jams with gold trimmed red terra cotta molding.

The entry portico is flanked by two wide terrazzo stair cases that connect the upper floors of the building to the foyer. It utilizes windows in the tower to provide natural lighting to the stairwell.

The Class of 1971 had the school's seal, a representation of the Will Rogers cattle ranch brand, set into the terrazzo floor.

The bronze bust of Will Rogers, a gift from the class of 1945, rests on a marble pedestal in a terra cotta inset covered with a gold leaf floral pattern.

The picture on the left shows the doors to the old gymnasium. The doors are inset in a niche with a red terra cotta mantle including a clock topped with a medallion. Notice the art deco border of the floor and the decorative hanging lamps used to light the gym foyer.

The Main Hall

The main hallway, connecting the east and west foyers, is lit by decorative hanging lamps identical to those in the main building. The hallway is covered by 9,892 terra cotta tiles, inset display windows and commemorative plaques. Notice the fine ornamental ceiling molding with a decorative repeating floral pattern.

One of my favorite features at Will Rogers is the water fountain in the main hall. Take a moment to appreciate the fine detail and craftsmanship. The water fountains are inset in an art deco styled recess with red terra cotta tiles. Two vertical tile sections have a vertical fluted pattern that is capped with a gold leaf design.

The doorways to the offices on the south side of the main hallway are intricately designed. The main office entrance doors are inset from the corridor walls and framed with red terra cotta tiles.

The tiled frame has rounded vertically fluted sides that rise to a decorative panel above the doors. Directly above the doors and beneath the capital panel is the tiled upper door frame sheet that displays "OFFICE" in gold. Above the doorway frame is a matching mandarin red art deco designed panel. The terra cotta panel has a gold leaf floral design that surrounds a protruding red medallion accentuated with a gold design.

Lining the main hall are lighted trophy cases that were added in the 1950's. Inset in the wall, they display student and faculty awards, achievements and post notices of upcoming events. Fluted vertical terra cotta panels embellish the cases.

The Library

Entry to the library is through one of twin inset doorways. The entrance hall is between two large fluted round columns. The ceiling molding provides a sharp contrast to the red terra cotta tile. Above the doors, embossed in gold, is "Library" in a terra cotta panel identical to the one over the main office doors.

There is a sharp contrast between the main hallway and the design of the library. The library uses soft pastel colors contrasted with walnut-stained book cases and interior framing. The central hallway is bold, elegant and vibrant whereas the library is quiet and serene.

The room has ample natural light showing through the wall of windows at the rear of the room. Additional lighting is provided by hanging art deco lights.

The library is divided in half by a progression of columned archways. Each half of the room has a different color scheme. As one enters the library, the south side is painted a light green pastel. The north half of the library (toward the windows) is a light blue pastel. Notice how the molding is beautifully shaped over the room dividing archways.

Exquisite crown molding is used throughout the library. The wood molding and trim is painted light beige, brown and gold. The ceiling molding incorporates an art deco fan design between fluted molding.

East Foyer

The foyer on the east end of the main hall is used as the primary public entrance and has a security desk for visitor sign in. The east foyer connects to the auditorium foyer, exterior portico and the hall of Will Rogers' photos. The area is designed similar to the west foyer, but it is not as large or elegant. The door under the clock opens directly to the auditorium.

The floral design hanging over the auditorium foyer doors is replicated in the main hallway. The auditorium doors feature a vintage clock embedded in a red terra cotta frame.

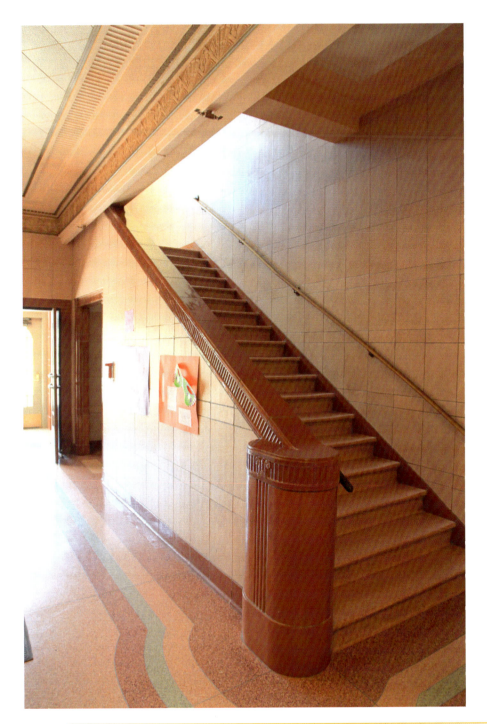

The foyer has a pair of stairs connecting it, through the east tower, to classrooms in the above floors. The stairs include the same curved terra cotta base, fluted trim and brass rails as the west foyer. However, the east stairwell is much narrower.

Auditorium Foyer

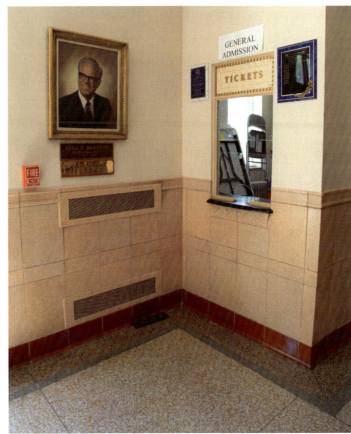

The auditorium foyer has a light tan and green-gray design that is more subdued and less elegant than the main school entrances. The ceiling trim has elaborate molding with fans and floral design.

The lobby is illuminated by natural light from three pairs of deco-designed glass doors. The doors are identical to the east and west tower entry doors. Additional lighting is provided by two different styles of hanging deco lights.

Auditorium

The auditorium is more ornate, decorative and artistic than most high school auditoriums. The stage is framed by terra cotta tile pilasters topped by an elaborately designed mantel with a floral and fan design. The stage has stair cases on each side creating a protruded section of stage in front. The front of the stage has ornamental brass vents embedded in the red terra cotta tile.

The auditorium seats 1533 people and has a full balcony. It still has the original 1930's cast iron framed wooden seats.

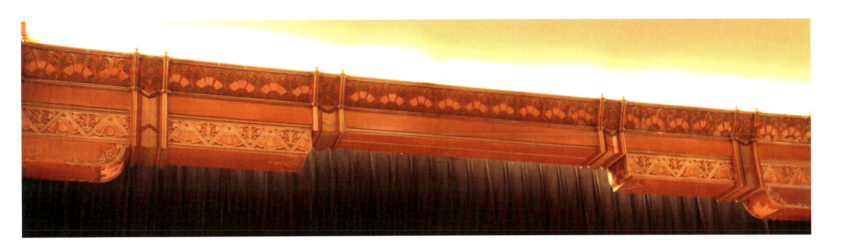

Koberling brought in a nationally known interior decorator, Alexander Rindskopf, to design the Will Rogers' auditorium and other key public areas, including the entry vestibules and library. In the auditorium he chose red terra cotta with ivory and gold detailing for the color scheme. The walls are tan with dark blue drapes on the stage and windows.

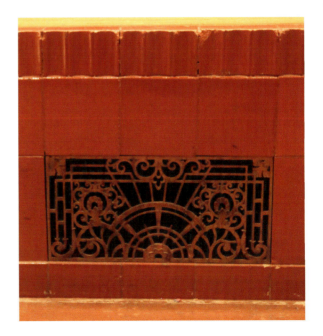

On each side of the stage (see right page) are three artistically designed wall panels. The center panel has a false balcony, which compliments the theatrical atmosphere, with fan styled grill works that cover air conditioning equipment, air vents and speakers. On each side of the center panel is a section with three-twenty foot vertical light sconces. The floral-fan designed molding and unique custom designed lamps underneath the balcony provide a beautiful theater setting.

Auditorium Balcony and Floor

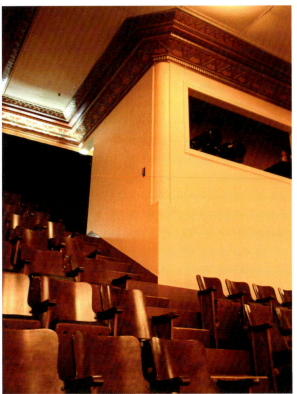

The auditorium balcony has a special charm all its own. The molding as usual is magnificent and large art deco styled lights illuminate the veranda. Centered at the top of the balcony is a control room for spot lights and audio video control equipment.

The Rindskopf Mural

The artistic elements of the auditorium, including the mural, were designed and painted by Chicago artist, Alex C. Rindskoph. In the center of the mural are three stanzas from the poem "The Kansas Immigrants" by John Greenleaf Whittier.

The Rindskopf Mural

The most striking feature of the auditorium is the Rindskopf Mural. Standing 33 feet tall, it depicts the immigration of white settlers to Indian territory. In the center of the mural is a verse from the poem, "The Kansas Immigrants" by John Greenleaf Whittier.

Alexander Rindskopf, the interior designer for the Auditorium, proposed a huge wall mural and recommended Native American artist, Acee Blue Eagle, for the project. When the school board put the project up for bid, Rindskopf was the only one to submit a proposal for the job.

The mural project did not have funding. It was anticipated that the project would have to be funded after the initial construction. Joseph Koberling, recognizing the value of the mural, accumulated savings from other projects in the building to raise the $10,000 required. Thus it was included in the original building.

The Kansas Immigrants
by
John Greenleaf Whittier

We cross the Prairie as of old
The pilgrims crossed the sea.
To make the West, as they the East.
The homestead of the free.

We're flowing from our native hills
As our free rivers flow:
The blessing of our Mother-land
Is on us as we go.

We go to plant our common schools
On distant prairie swells.
And give the Sabbaths of the wild
The music of her bells.

Famous Will Rogers Alumni

Many Will Rogers graduates have gone on to establish themselves nationally. They include such people as :

Don Chandler (1934-2011), Class of '52
Chandler was an All-Pro professional football player with the New York Giants and Green Bay Packers. He is one of the best punters of all time and led the NFL in average yards per punt in 1957 and led the league with a field goal percentage of 67.9 percent in 1962. Chandler still holds the record for most field goals scored in a Super Bowl with four in the 1968 Super Bowl. Chandler helped Vince Lombardi's Green Bay Packers win Super Bowls I and II.

Charles Bell (1935–1995), Class of '53
Although not a formally trained artist, Bell became a prominent San Francisco studio artist who focused on paintings of vintage toys, pinball machines and dolls arranged in various positions.

John C. (Jack) Oxley, Class of 55
As a racehorse owner and breeder, Oxley's horse "Monarchos" won the 2001 Kentucky Derby. He also owned "Beautiful Pleasure," 1999 winner of the Breeders' Cup. In the 1970's, Oxley helped establish the Oxley Nature Center in Tulsa's Mohawk park.

Silkscreen Paper Circus Act, by Charles Bell 1995

Johnny Sellers Class of 55
Sellers rode in six Kentucky Derbys. He won the 1961 Derby and the Preakness riding "Carry Back." That year, he won eight straight races and ended the year as the United States Champion Jockey and was featured on the August 28, 1961 Sports Illustrated cover.

Russell Myers, Class of '56
Meyers is creator of the nationally syndicated comic strip, Broom-Hilda. The first strip was published and syndicated by the Chicago Tribune on April 19, 1970. He was the "National Cartoonists Society's Best Humor Strip Award" winner for 1975.

David Gates, Class of '58
Gates is a successful singer/ song writer who was the lead singer with "Bread" and had numerous hits.

Anita Bryant, Class of '58
Bryant was second runner-up in the 1959 Miss America beauty pageant. This led to a singing and performance career. She had 11 songs reach the "U.S. Hot 100" list. She was the television spokesperson for the Florida Citrus Commission until becoming a national anti-gay rights activist.

Leon Russell, Class of '59
Russell was known in high school as Claude Russell Bridges. He began his musical career at 14, lying about his age to land gigs playing backup at Tulsa nightclubs. Russell is a singer, songwriter, pianist, and guitarist. He has played with: Jerry Lee Lewis, Phil Spector, Elton John and The Rolling Stones. He plays multiple genres including rock, blues, and gospel. During the 1960's and 1970's, Russell owned the Church Recording Studio on 3rd Street in Tulsa.

Elvin Bishop, Class of '60
Bishop is a blues guitarist with over 18 albums. He has played with: "The Allman Brothers Band " and B.B. King. Charlie Daniels immortalized Elvin in song; "Elvin Bishop sittin' on a bale of hay; he ain't good lookin', but he sure can play". From the 1975 song "The South's Gonna Do It"

Ron Radford, Class of '62
Radford is hailed around the world as a master flamenco guitarist who received training from Carlos Montoya in New York after graduating from the University of Tulsa. Ron also studied under Andres Segovia. Ron is the only individual ever to be awarded a Fulbright Scholarship in flamenco guitar. He is one of the world's most successful flamenco musicians.

Gailard Sartain, Class of '63
Before becoming a comedic performer, Sartain was a successful artist and illustrator having done the record cover designs for Leon Russell's "Will O' the Wisp" album and illustrations for nationally published magazines. He became a Tulsa TV legend creating the iconic Dr. Mazeppa Pompazoidi on his KOTV weekly program, "Uncanny Film Festival and Camp Meeting." The program featured "Saturday Night Live" like skits that were written and performed by Sartain, Gary Busey and Sherman Oaks.

Sartain appeared in over 50 motion pictures, but is best know for his regular appearances for 20 years on the popular country comedy and music show Hee Haw.

Gailard Sartain from the TV show Hee Haw

Dave Rader, Class of '75
Rader was a quarterback for the University of Tulsa football team. He was the starting quarterback in 1977 and 1978 and was the 11th round draft pick of the San Diego Chargers and later played for the New York Giants.

He was the head football coach of the University of Tulsa Golden Hurricane from 1988 to 1999. He then served as the Offensive Coordinator at the University of Alabama 2003 to 2006. In 2010, Dave served as co-offensive coordinator and quarterback coach at the University of Mississippi.

John Ward (1948 – 2012) Class of '66
Ward was an outstanding football player who was a first round draft pick out of Oklahoma State University in 1970 by the Minnesota Vikings. He played seven years in the NFL.

Lee Mayberry, Class of '88
Mayberry led the Ropers to the 1988 state basketball championship. He played basketball at the University of Arkansas and helped lead them to the 1990 Final Four. He was a first round draft choice of the Milwaukee Bucks. Mayberry played professionally from 1992–1999.

S.E. Hinton & *"The Outsiders"*

Matt Dillon and S.E. Hinton, Walt Disney Productions © 1982

> "If you want to be a writer, I have two pieces of advice. One is to be a reader. I think that's one of the most important parts of learning to write. The other piece of advice is `Just do it!' Don't think about it, don't agonize, sit down and write."
>
> . . .   S.E. Hinton

Susan Eloise Hinton - Class of '66

At the age of 15, Susan was a freshman at Will Rogers. When a friend was beaten after going to a movie, she wrote "*The Outsiders*", a story based on the conflict of two rival male gangs at Rogers.

The mother of a friend read the manuscript and contacted a New York publishing agent on her behalf. Viking Publishing signed her to a contract and printed the initial edition of the book, "The Outsiders" in 1967,

Initially the book was not a big success, but librarians and teachers promoted the book as teen relevant literature and the book became a best seller. Today it is one of the most popular adolescent books printed and has been in continuous print since its beginnings. The book has sold 13 million copies and still sells over 500,000 copies a year.

Hinton uses her initials instead of her full name because the publishers feared reviewers of "The Outsiders." wouldn't value the writing of a young girl.

The story of "The Outsiders" is the struggle between two competing gangs: the "Greasers" and the "Socs", pronounced sosh-ez, short for *socialites*. This was a typical social class conflict expressed through the perspectives of high school students.

The works of Hinton include:

- The Outsiders (1967), (movie 1983)
- That Was Then, This Is Now (1971) (movie 1985)
- Rumble Fish (1975) (movie 1983)
- Tex (1979) (movie 1982)
- Taming the Star Runner (1988)
- *Big David, Little David* (Children's Book)
- *The Puppy Sister* (Children's Book)
- *Hawkes Harbor* (2004)
- *Some of Tim's Stories* (2007)

"The Outsiders" Movie (1983, 2005)

The movie was directed by Francis Ford Coppola. One of the producers of the film was Gray Frederickson, producer of "The Godfather" (1972), "The Godfather: Part II" (1974) and "Apocalypse Now" (1979). The film score was composed by Francis Ford Coppola's father, Francis Coppola. The main movie theme, "Stay Gold", was performed by Stevie Wonder.

"The Outsiders" served as a vehicle to stardom for many young actors: Rob Lowe, Tom Cruise, C. Thomas Howell, Patrick Swayze, Emilio Estevez, Matt Dillon, Ralph Macchio and Diane Lane were all featured in the film.

Will Rogers alum, Gailard Sartain (Class of '63), also had a small part in the film. He played Jerry, a school teacher, responsible for the children at the abandoned church.

The movie was filmed in Tulsa and several prominent landmarks are shown in the film. A fight scene was filmed in Crutchfield Park located at 1345 E. Independence. Other scenes were filmed at the Admiral Twin and in front of the Boston Avenue Methodist Church.

In 2005, Coppola edited the original film. He added additional footage and new music to update the film for new viewers. It was released on DVD, as "The Outsiders: The Complete Novel." Coppola re-inserted some deleted scenes to make the film closer to the written novel.

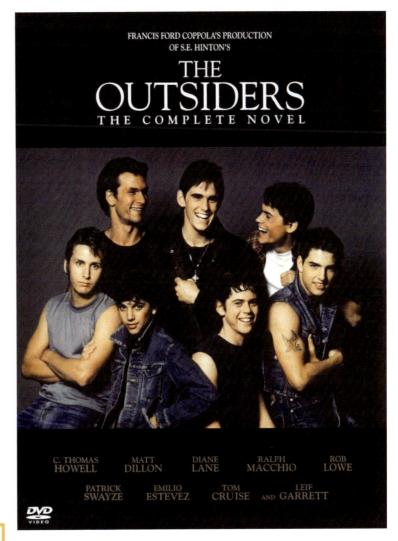

Regarding "The Outsiders" cast (1983):
"I was a mother to all of them, and I wouldn't take any guff from any of them. If one of them acted up, I'd crack the whip and say, 'I'm going to cut your lines.' They were these goofy teenage boys, no adult guidance, no nothing.
They wore me out. "
S.E. Hinton

Note!

I attended WR during the period the story is set and although I remember the "Greasers" and the "Socs" groups, I don't recall the degree of violence portrayed in the novel.

Don Wagner

Ride on... to excellence!

Will Rogers High School Community Foundation

The Mission of the WRHS Community Foundation is to empower the students of WRCHS by expanding and enhancing educational opportunities, and to engage staff, families and community by providing enriching experiences and programs.

Learn more about the Foundation at www.willrogersfoundation.net

Will Rogers Community Foundation Hall of Fame

1989
Anita Bryant (Dry), 1958
Gordona Moore Duca, 1958
David Gates, 1958
S.E. Hinton, 1966
Ernest Moody, 1944
David Rader, 1975
Rodger Randle, 1962

1992
Ronald Radford, 1962

2009
Phillip N. Butler, 1956
James D. Dunn, 1960
James W. Jones, MD, PhD, 1959
William L. Lewis, 1949
Carol Walsh Morsani, 1949
Frank L. Morsani, 1949
Leon Russell (fka Russell Bridges), 1959
Gailard Sartain, 1963
Robert J. Stuart, 1944

2011
Preston C. Caruthers, 1945
Stephen D. Chesebro', 1959
Lee Mayberry, 1988
Russell B. Myers, 1956

2012
Nancy Jo Daulton Beier, 1956
Elvin Bishop, 1960
Donald "Babe" Chandler, 1952
Paul Davis, 1955
Warren G. Guntheroth, MD, 1945
H. Thomas Harrison, DMin, 1972
Fred Sanders, 1945
Neil R. Sparks, Jr., 1954

2013
Lynette Bennett (Danskin), 1955
Linda Chambers Bradshaw, 1960
Paula Combest Unruh, 1947
Richard B. Counts, MD, 1959
Gordon Morgan, 1953
Janet Wright Kizziar, 1957
James W. Russell, PhD, 1962

Will Rogers Alumni Websites

Class	Website
1942	http://classreport.org/usa/ok/tulsa/wrhs/1942
1956	http://wrhs1956.com/
1957	http://wrhs57.com/
1958	http://www.willrogers1958.com/
1959	http://willrogers1959.com/
1960	http://www.wrhs1960.com/
1961	http://classreport.org/usa/ok/tulsa/wrhs/1961/
1962	http://www.classreport.org/usa/ok/tulsa/wrhs/1962
1963	http://willrogers1963.com/
1965	http://www.facebook.com/groups/1391369734413472/
1966	http://wrhs1966.com/
1967	http://wrhs67.com/
1969	http://www.wrhs69.com/
1971	http://willrogershs1971.tripod.com/
1973	http://www.facebook.com/groups/226783510669112/
1974	http://www.facebook.com/groups/565375520185131/
1977	http://willrogers1977.com/
1978	http://www.facebook.com/groups/1386062734947925/
1980	http://www.facebook.com/groups/163883637130372/?ref=br_rs
1983	http://www.facebook.com/groups/518900578163888/
1984	http://www.facebook.com/groups/576948609010188/
1987	http://www.facebook.com/groups/544789878915051/
1988	http://www.facebook.com/groups/593725040649205/
1989	http://willrogers89.com/
1992	http://www.facebook.com/groups/409356742517390/
1993	http://www.facebook.com/groups/154095224780903/
1994	http://www.facebook.com/groups/263794880427837/
1995	http://www.facebook.com/groups/529411833774550/
1997	http://www.facebook.com/groups/681669355181003/
1998	http://myspace.com/wrhs98
1999	http://www.facebook.com/groups/606691832708273/

Will Rogers High School Community Foundation
WWW.WillRogersFoundation.NET

Will Rogers High School All Sports Booster Club
(Contact Will Rogers High School to become involved)

Will Rogers High School Alumni Foundation
PO Box 4282 Tulsa, OK 74159-0282 : Phone: 918-835-8674

National Register of Historic Places

In November of 2004, Betty Ann (Brown) Trinka, Class of 55, began the process to add Will Rogers High School to the prestigious National Register of Historic Places.

> "People in the alumni association told me there was no way it could be done. I just didn't believe it, because the school is just so beautiful. The art deco architecture is so fabulous and it has been kept in great condition."
>
> Betty Ann (Brown) Trinka

According to Betty, she tried to get assistance for funding the project from school alumni organizations and classmates to no avail. She was told by the Tulsa Historical Society and the State Historical Society that submitting a NRHP application for Will Rogers High School was a waste of time. Betty dealt with naysayers and persisted with her convictions by funding the project herself.

Betty contracted Cathy Ambler, of Preservation Oklahoma, to research and prepare the nomination documents. The application was submitted to the National Park Service July 24, 2007. The 85 page National Park Service Registration Form is a wonderful description of Will Rogers High School and includes:
- History of the School
- Architectural Assessment
- Drawings and Diagrams
- Photographs (by Cathy and Allen Ambler)

After three years of persistence and hard work, the application was submitted. On September 9, 2007, Betty's dream became a reality. Will Rogers High School was certified as a National Historic Place, with national significance.

You can review the actual NRHP application at:
http://www.cr.nps.gov/nr/feature/school/2011/Will_Rogers_High_School.htm

Nationally Significant

Although there are over 1,200 Oklahoma listings on the National Register of Historic Places, Will Rogers is one of less than sixty to be recognized as having national significance. The others have a state or local classification. The National Park Service has stated "Will Rogers High School is one of the best examples of Art Deco high school architecture in the United States."

Importance of NRHP

Being added to the National Register of Historic Places as a national landmark is an important accomplishment and has had substantial positive consequences for Will Rogers High School.

Betty Ann (Brown) Trinka & Principal Kevin Burr
Picture courtesy of Tulsa World

The award broadens the appreciation and pride of all Tulsans and especially the Tulsa Public School System. The local recognition and publicity brought by being declared a national landmark no doubt saved the school from being closed and eventually sold as proposed in 2011.

> Will Rogers High School was listed in the National Register on September 6, 2007.
> It was listed under National Register Criteria A and C, and its NRIS number is 07000918.

Restoration & Improvement Projects

Historic Restoration

Being added to the National Register of Historic Places led to a commitment by the Tulsa School Board to restoring and maintaining this historically relevant building. This included the restoration of damaged terra cotta, the replacement of the south side entry doors, and the replacement of almost nine hundred vintage inefficient windows. A bond issue in 2010, funded the renovation project that was performed by Fritz Baily Architects and Trigon General Contractors.

The original 1939 windows were steel-framed, single-paned, windows that were by today's standards, highly inefficient. Some of the old windows had been painted blue to provide shade but degraded the building's appearance. The new dual-paned replacement windows are tinted and 50% more energy efficient. The new windows have resulted in a 14% decrease in the school's energy costs. The new windows also have noise abatement properties that improve the classroom environment.

Every effort was made to restore the building to its original beauty, while at the same time modernizing the efficiency and functionality. The new windows were carefully designed and assembled to match the original windows' appearance. The door replacements were designed to replicate the appearance of the original doors and the terra cotta repairs are blended in so well that one can't easily distinguish them from the original work.

A new cafeteria was added that features an outside eating area for the students. The old cafeteria was converted into two lecture halls.

Will Rogers College High School

Change to Con-Current Enrollment School

In 2011, Will Rogers High School became a dual enrollment school with a college and/or career ready curriculum. The school consists of grades 7 through 12 eliminating the middle school / high school separation. Will Rogers, in cooperation with Tulsa Community College (TCC), created a program where a student can earn up to 6 college units per semester, tuition free, during their junior and senior years. This is equivalent to earning an associate degree concurrent with a high school diploma. The graduating class of 2014, the first since the school was reorganized, had seniors earning between 6 and 30 college credit hours. Transfer of TCC credits are accepted by the University of Tulsa, University of Oklahoma and Oklahoma State University.

> "The key to our advisory program is building relationships between students and staff. Students stay with the same advisor through their time at Will Rogers College High School, which gives students a constant contact who can help them academically and with career and postsecondary education exploration."
>
> **By Michael Ballard, former Vice Principal, oversees the WRAP program**

Students who live in the neighborhoods surrounding Will Rogers have the right to attend the school provided they agree to abide by and participate in the school's programs. The rest of the student body is selected by a lottery of applicants divided equally among the four quadrants of the Tulsa Public School District.

The Will Rogers curriculum sets a higher standard than most Tulsa high schools. The goals are to: reduce the drop out rate, graduate academically college ready students and provide the availability of college credit courses.

To accomplish these goals traditional Junior High (years 7-9) and Senior High (years 10-12) have been integrated into a single school. This allows supervision of the educational development on an individual basis for a more extended period of time. For example special instruction is given to young students whose first language isn't English so they will be prepared to succeed in later grades.

The Will Rogers Advisement Program (WRAP) was created to build relationships between the school, parents and students. It provides academic and career guidance. WRAP makes available weekly advisory periods where teachers meet with groups of students to teach academic and learning skills and discus career and social issues.

New Field House - north side of school

Will Rogers Public Tours

Since 2009, Will Rogers High School has opened its doors for public tours. This Is a result of the efforts of Steve Wright and others to raise awareness of the fine art deco architecture and the significant historic and artistic holdings within the school.

The tour that I attended several years ago began with a presentation in the auditorium about the history of the school and its namesake, Will Rogers. They spoke of the fine craftsmanship that implemented the architectural designs of the school.

After a thirty minute presentation, the audience was invited to join one of many tour groups being led by alumni and student docents. They guided people through the halls describing the various highlights. People were encouraged to take pictures. Visitors enjoyed the auditorium, library and particularly the hall of large Will Rogers' photographs.

I thought having students act as docents was a brilliant idea. It taught them about the history and traditions of both Will Rogers the school and the man. Learning the value of the craftsmanship, materials and art works through the school teaches them to respect and care for the school.

The tours accomplish many things:

- It showcases an Art Deco masterpiece
- Generates pride of the school by students
- Alumni reconnect with the school
- Generates community outreach
- School is kept in pristine condition
- The tours recognize Will Rogers High School as a National Historic Place, with national significance

In 2009, Steve Wright (Class of 56) started a program to develop public awareness of the Will Rogers High School's history and traditions. He wanted people to enjoy and appreciate the artistic beauty and craftsmanship that went into the construction of the building. For these reasons and others he promoted a public tour of the high school.

He was told he could use the auditorium for a presentation, but not too expect much of a crowd since interest in the school was perceived as being low. Several hundred people turned out for the initial presentation and tour.

Call the school for upcoming tour dates.

Recommended Data Sources

Will Rogers College High School Website
http://rogers.tulsaschools.org/

National Register of Historic Places Application
http://www.cr.nps.gov/nr/feature/school/2011/Will_Rogers_High_School.htm

Will Rogers Foundation Website
http://willrogersfoundation.net/

Ride On
http://issuu.com/dickrisk/docs/ride_on__for_web/1

Tulsa 1942: LIFE, Eisenstaedt visit Tulsa high schools
http://www.batesline.com/archives/2012/09/tulsa-1942-life-eisenstaedt-visi.html

Will Rogers makes the A-list
http://www.tulsaworld.com/archives/will-rogers-makes-the-a-list/article_ddfaad19-9624-504e-b72d-12704f4a55e3.html

Will Rogers Completes Window Replacement Project
http://www.ktul.com/story/18968624/will-rogers-high-school-completes-window-replacement-project

Tulsa Art Deco Top 10 - (See Page 80)
www.Tulsa-Books.com

Tulsa Art Deco Experience - (See Page 80)
www.Tulsa-Books.com

Tulsa Art Deco
Tulsa Foundation for Architecture

Will Rogers High School Wikipedia
http://en.wikipedia.org/wiki/Will_Rogers_High_School

Will Rogers Memorial Museum Website
http://www.willrogers.com/

WRHS Pictorial History
http://willrogers1977.com/blog/wrhs-pictorial-history/

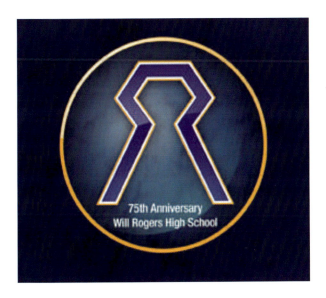

Sorry for any errors!
When collecting information there is always the potential for errors. Diligent effort has been made to verify the information printed in this book. Any errors or omissions were unintentional. If you have constructive suggestions you can email me at:

Don.Wagner.OK@gmail.com.

, Don Wagner

Tulsa Books

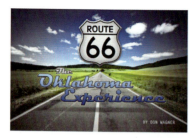

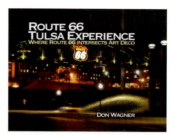
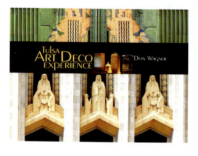
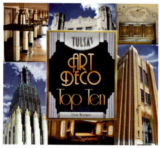
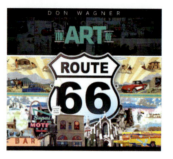

Tulsa 1960's

Tulsa 1960's (Available Oct. 2014)

Our coffee table books provide an entertaining and informative guide through:

- Art Deco
- Route 66
- Tulsa
- History

Our books are photographic journals with pertinent history and an abundance of interesting facts.

Oklahoma Tourist Guides Inc.
www.Tulsa-Books.com
(918) 693-1198
DON.WAGNER.OK@GMAIL.COM

Our Books Available at:

Made In Oklahoma
Gilcrease Museum Gift Shop
Lyons Indian / Tulsa Treasures
Dwelling Spaces
Ziegler's
Ida Red
Tulsa J. Hallmark Stores
Will Rogers Memorial (Claremore)
River Spirit Casino Gift Shop
Goodwill Store on Southwest Blvd.
www.amazon.com